Computerised Accounting Practice Set
Using Xero Online Accounting

Expert Level

This expert level computerised accounting practice set is for students who need to practice exercises of Xero Online Accounting, students can record a month's transactions of Richmond Papers Pty Ltd and can create financial reports.

It covers the following topics.

- Setting Up a New Accounting System
- Suppliers, Purchases and Inventory
- Customers, Sales and Inventory
- Receipts, Payments and Expenses
- Bank Reconciliation
- Financial Reports

Syed Tirmizi
Certified Advisor

ISBN 978-0-9945988-4-4

9 780994 598844 >

Part A
Practice Set

This page is blank.

Instructions

You have recently been appointed as an Accounts Assistant at Richmond Papers Pty Ltd, a new business dealing in printing and publishing. Your responsibilities are to set up a computerised accounting system, update the company records and produce financial reports.

The company started trading on 1st April 2016. All documents have been checked for accuracy and owner of the business, John Smith has authorised these documents.

The company uses straight line method for depreciating its non-current assets at 10% yearly. The policy defines the decline in value of these non-current assets on monthly basis.

You are required to complete the following tasks for April 2016 in the order given.

- a) Setting Up a New Accounting System
- b) Suppliers, Purchases and Inventory
- c) Customers, Sales and Inventory
- d) Receipts, Payments and Expenses
- e) Bank Reconciliation
- f) Financial Reports

a) Setting Up a New Accounting System

Create a new company in Xero Online Accounting using the following information.

Company Name	Richmond Papers Pty Ltd
ABN	46 995 263 632
Address	23 High Street
	Richmond
	VIC 3121
Phone Number	03 9988 7766
Current Financial Year	Jul 2015 – Jun 2016

Set up Suppliers, Customers and Inventory with the help of Tables 1, 2 and 3.

Additional Information

i.   On April 1st 2016, $25,000 Capital was introduced by the owner of the business and was paid into the Bank Current Account. The reference for this transaction is CR0001.

ii.   On April 2nd 2016, the Company purchased a motor vehicle from Western Motors for $12,000 + $1,200 GST. Cheque number 000001 was used to make the settlement.

iii.   At the end of the month depreciation on the motor vehicle and bank service charges are to be recorded to the relevant accounts.

Table 1: Suppliers

Supplier Account Details	
Mark & Tony 41 Middlesbrough Road St Albans - VIC 3021 Contact Name: Sue Hawkins Email: sales@mt.com.au	Telephone: 03 9876 5432 Sales Settings: Tax Inclusive Purchase Settings: Tax Inclusive ABN: 84 678 592 583 Payment Terms: 30 day(s) after the invoice date
David & Sons 67 Longwood Road Craigieburn - VIC 3064 Contact Name: John Alexander Email: sales@ds.com.au	Telephone: 03 9765 4321 Sales Settings: Tax Inclusive Purchase Settings: Tax Inclusive ABN: 65 473 985 624 Payment Terms: 30 day(s) after the invoice date
Ian & Co Pty Ltd 94 High Street Fitzroy - VIC 3065 Contact Name: Angela Samson Email: sales@ic.com.au	Telephone: 03 9654 3210 Sales Settings: Tax Inclusive Purchase Settings: Tax Inclusive ABN: 25 657 917 634 Payment Terms: 30 day(s) after the invoice date
Smith & Baker 11 Westfield Road Lalor - VIC 3075 Contact Name: Andrew Smith Email: sales@sb.com.au	Telephone: 03 9543 2109 Sales Settings: Tax Inclusive Purchase Settings: Tax Inclusive ABN: 54 637 945 746 Payment Terms: 30 day(s) after the invoice date
Gary Corporation 94 Wellington Street Preston - VIC 3072 Contact Name: Adam Miller Email: sales@gc.com.au	Telephone: 03 9432 1098 Sales Settings: Tax Inclusive Purchase Settings: Tax Inclusive ABN: 74 325 496 324 Payment Terms: 30 day(s) after the invoice date
East End Pty Ltd 34 Canterbury Road Epping - VIC 3076 Contact Name: Nick Abbey Email: sales@ee.com.au	Telephone: 03 9321 0987 Sales Settings: Tax Inclusive Purchase Settings: Tax Inclusive ABN: 96 376 843 587 Payment Terms: 30 day(s) after the invoice date

Table 2: Customers

Customer Account Details	
Peter Electronics 9 Western Avenue Brooklyn - VIC 3012 Contact Name: Megan Boucher Email: info@pe.com.au	Telephone: 03 9123 4567 Sales Settings: Tax Inclusive Purchase Settings: Tax Inclusive ABN: 52 639 846 324 Payment Terms: 30 day(s) after the invoice date
Western Estate Agents 362 High Street Sunshine - VIC 3029 Contact Name: Ashley Champ Email: info@wea.com.au	Telephone: 03 9234 5678 Sales Settings: Tax Inclusive Purchase Settings: Tax Inclusive ABN: 47 528 963 764 Payment Terms: 30 day(s) after the invoice date
Surf Stores 54 Dundee Street Deer Park - VIC 3023 Contact Name: Natalie Dunn Email: info@ss.com.au	Telephone: 03 9345 6789 Sales Settings: Tax Inclusive Purchase Settings: Tax Inclusive ABN: 95 768 359 862 Payment Terms: 30 day(s) after the invoice date
Sally's Warehouse 12 Wood Street Essendon - VIC 3040 Contact Name: George Gordon Email: info@sw.com.au	Telephone: 03 9456 7890 Sales Settings: Tax Inclusive Purchase Settings: Tax Inclusive ABN: 76 662 485 964 Payment Terms: 30 day(s) after the invoice date
Horizon Designs 32 Abbots Road Broadmeadows - VIC 3047 Contact Name: Lee Hopkins Email: info@hd.com.au	Telephone: 03 9567 8901 Sales Settings: Tax Inclusive Purchase Settings: Tax Inclusive ABN: 12 528 972 562 Payment Terms: 30 day(s) after the invoice date
Thomson Clothings 84 Spring Street Thomastown - VIC 3074 Contact Name: Alston Leeson Email: info@thc.com.au	Telephone: 03 9678 9012 Sales Settings: Tax Inclusive Purchase Settings: Tax Inclusive ABN: 74 635 842 321 Payment Terms: 30 day(s) after the invoice date
Globe Travels Pty Ltd 42 Barry Road Melbourne - VIC 3000 Contact Name: Robert Nickelson Email: info@gt.com.au	Telephone: 03 9789 0123 Sales Settings: Tax Inclusive Purchase Settings: Tax Inclusive ABN: 85 365 412 741 Payment Terms: 30 day(s) after the invoice date
Tiffany Cakes 36 High Road Williamstown - VIC 3016 Contact Name: Anthony Robins Email: info@tc.com.au	Telephone: 03 9890 1234 Sales Settings: Tax Inclusive Purchase Settings: Tax Inclusive ABN: 78 635 254 524 Payment Terms: 30 day(s) after the invoice date

Table 3: Inventory

Inventory Details	
Item Code: A3CP Item Name & Description: A3 Copy Paper Track Account: 630-Inventory Selling Price: $40 per Unit	COGS Account: 311 - COGS - A3 Copy Paper Tax Rate: GST on Expenses Sales Account: 201 - Sales - A3 Copy Paper Tax Rate: GST on Income
Item Code: A4CP Item Name & Description: A4 Copy Paper Track Account: 630-Inventory Selling Price: $15 per Unit	COGS Account: 312 - COGS - A4 Copy Paper Tax Rate: GST on Expenses Sales Account: 202 - Sales - A4 Copy Paper Tax Rate: GST on Income
Item Code: A5CP Item Name & Description: A5 Copy Paper Track Account: 630-Inventory Selling Price: $14 per Unit	COGS Account: 313 - COGS - A5 Copy Paper Tax Rate: GST on Expenses Sales Account: 203 - Sales – A5 Copy Paper Tax Rate: GST on Income
Item Code: COLO Item Name & Description: Coloured Paper Track Account: 630-Inventory Selling Price: $20 per Unit	COGS Account: 314 - COGS - Coloured Paper Tax Rate: GST on Expenses Sales Account: 204 - Sales - Coloured Paper Tax Rate: GST on Income
Item Code: EN01 Item Name & Description: Envelopes Large Track Account: 630-Inventory Selling Price: $35 per Unit	COGS Account: 315 - COGS - Envelopes Large Tax Rate: GST on Expenses Sales Account: 205 - Sales -Envelopes Large Tax Rate: GST on Income
Item Code: RR18 Item Name & Description: Register Rolls Track Account: 630-Inventory Selling Price: $54 per Unit	COGS Account: 316 - COGS - Register Rolls Tax Rate: GST on Expenses Sales Account: 206 - Sales - Register Rolls Tax Rate: GST on Income

b) Suppliers, Purchases and Inventory

Enter the following purchase invoices and purchase returns into the computer.

Purchase Invoices

Date	Supplier	Ref. No.	Item	Description	Qty	Cost	Gross Amt Inc GST
April 2nd	Gary Corporation	412	A3CP	A3 Copy Paper	200	$25.00	$5,000.00
April 2nd	Smith & Baker	G/749	A5CP	A5 Copy Paper	250	$8.00	$2,000.00
April 4th	Ian & Co. Pty Ltd	00854	A4CP	A4 Copy Paper	500	$8.00	$4,000.00
April 5th	David & Sons	2016-18	RR18	Register Rolls	350	$38.00	$13,300.00
April 7th	Mark & Tony	A423	COLO	Coloured Paper	200	$14.00	$2,800.00
April 9th	East End Pty Ltd	EE2141	EN01	Envelopes Large	200	$22.00	$4,400.00

Purchase Returns

Date	Supplier	Ref. No.	Item	Description	Qty	Cost	Gross Amt Inc GST
April 4th	Smith & Baker	G/749	A5CP	A5 Copy Paper	20	$8.00	$160.00
April 11th	David & Sons	2016-18	RR18	Register Rolls	25	$38.00	$950.00

c) Customers, Sales and Inventory

Enter the following sales invoices and sales returns into the computer.

Sales Invoices

Date	Customer	Inv. No.	Item	Description	Qty	Price	Amount Inc GST
April 5th	Horizon Designs	001	A4CP	A4 Copy Paper	70	$14.50	$1,015.00
			RR18	Register Rolls	60	$54.00	$3,240.00
			A5CP	A5 Copy Paper	70	$14.00	$980.00
						Total	$5,235.00
April 10th	Thomson Clothings	002	A4CP	A4 Copy Paper	60	$15.00	$900.00
			EN01	Envelopes Large	80	$35.00	$2,800.00
						Total	$3,700.00
April 12th	Globe Travels Pty Ltd	003	A4CP	A4 Copy Paper	60	$15.00	$900.00
			A3CP	A3 Copy Paper	50	$40.00	$2,000.00
			RR18	Register Rolls	70	$54.00	$3,780.00
			COLO	Coloured Paper	60	$20.00	$1,200.00
						Total	$7,880.00
April 14th	Tiffany Cakes	004	A4CP	A4 Copy Paper	50	$15.00	$750.00
			RR18	Register Rolls	60	$54.00	$3,240.00
			EN01	Envelopes Large	60	$35.00	$2,100.00
						Total	$6,090.00
April 19th	Peter Electronics	005	A4CP	A4 Copy Paper	60	$15.00	$900.00
			COLO	Coloured Paper	70	$20.00	$1,400.00
						Total	$2,300.00
April 21st	Sally's Warehouse	006	A4CP	A4 Copy Paper	70	$15.00	$1,050.00
			COLO	Coloured Paper	60	$20.00	$1,200.00
			A3CP	A3 Copy Paper	70	$40.00	$2,800.00
			RR18	Register Rolls	50	$54.00	$2,700.00
						Total	$7,750.00
April 25th	Western Estate Agents	007	A5CP	A5 Copy Paper	100	$14.00	$1,400.00
						Total	$1,400.00
April 27th	Surf Stores	008	A4CP	A4 Copy Paper	50	$15.00	$750.00
			RR18	Register Rolls	30	$54.00	$1,620.00
						Total	$2,370.00

Sales Returns

Date	Customer	Inv. No.	Item	Description	Qty	Price	Amount Inc GST
April 17th	Thomson Clothings	002	EN01	Envelopes Large	20	$35.00	$700.00
April 23rd	Sally's Warehouse	006	A4CP	A4 Copy Paper	10	$15.00	$150.00

d) Receipts, Payments and Expenses

Enter the following payments received from customers, payments made to suppliers and expenses into the computer.

Payments Received

Date	Receipt Type	Customer	Details	Amount ($)
April 13th	EFT	Horizon Designs	Invoice 001	$5,235.00
April 18th	Cheque	Thomson Clothings	Invoice 002	$3,000.00
April 20th	Cheque	Globe Travels Ltd	Invoice 003	$7,880.00
April 25th	EFT	Tiffany Cakes	Invoice 004	$6,090.00

Expenses Summary

Date	Cheque No.	Expenses	Details	Net	Tax	Gross ($)
April 2nd	000002	Rent	Richmond Real Estate	$1,000.00	$100.00	$1,100.00
April 7th	000003	Insurance Premium	Melbourne Insurance	$200.00	$20.00	$220.00
April 19th	000004	Electricity Bill	Victoria Electricity	$176.73	$17.67	$194.40
April 21st	000005	Telephone Bill	Australia Telecom	$196.92	$19.62	$215.84
April 26th	000006	Cleaning	Melbourne Removals	$50.00	$5.00	$55.00

Payments Made

Date	Cheque No.	Supplier	Details	Amount ($)
April 28th	000007	Gary Corporation	412	$5,000.00
April 28th	000008	Smith & Baker	G/749	$1,840.00

e) Bank Reconciliation

Prepare bank reconciliation for the month of April 2016. Company bank statement is as follows.

BANK OF RICHMOND

36 Spring Street, Richmond, VIC 3121   **Cheque Account Statement**

TEL 1800 AUSTRALIA   30-04-2016

Richmond Papers Pty Ltd
23 High Street
Richmond
VIC 3121

	BSB Number	Account Number
	123-456	987654321

Date	Details	Ref	Withdrawal	Deposits	Balance
01-Apr-16	Account opened - Initial deposit			$25,000.00	$25,000.00
02-Apr-16	CHQ 000001		$13,200.00		$11,800.00
02-Apr-16	CHQ 000002		$1,100.00		$10,700.00
07-Apr-16	CHQ 000003		$220.00		$10,480.00
13-Apr-16	EFT – Horizon Designs			$5,235.00	$15,715.00
18-Apr-16	Cheque deposited			$3,000.00	$18,715.00
19-Apr-16	CHQ 000004		$194.40		$18,520.60
20-Apr-16	Cheque deposited			$7,880.00	$26,400.60
21-Apr-16	CHQ 000005		$215.84		$26,184.76
22-Apr-16	CHQ 000007		$5,000.00		$21,184.76
25-Apr-16	EFT – Tiffany Cakes			$6,090.00	$27,274.76
30-Apr-16	Bank charges		$10.00		$27,264.76
	Totals		**$19,930.24**	**$47,205.00**	

f) Financial Reports

Print or save the following reports for the month of April 2016.

i.	Account Transactions
ii.	Inventory Item Summary
iii.	Bank Reconciliation Summary
iv.	Bank Statement
v.	Statement Exceptions
vi.	Statement of Cash Flows
vii.	Trial Balance
viii.	Profit & Loss
ix.	Balance Sheet

Part B

Solutions

This page is blank.

Account Transactions

Richmond Papers Pty Ltd
From 1 April 2016 to 30 April 2016

DATE	SOURCE	DESCRIPTION	REFERENCE	DEBIT	CREDIT	GROSS	GST
Accounts Payable							
Opening Balance					-		
2 Apr 2016	Payable Invoice	Gary Corporation	412		5,000.00	5,000.00	-
2 Apr 2016	Payable Invoice	Smith & Baker	G/749		2,000.00	2,000.00	-
4 Apr 2016	Payable Invoice	Ian & Co Pty Ltd	00854		4,000.00	4,000.00	-
4 Apr 2016	Payable Credit Note	Smith & Baker	G/749	160.00		(160.00)	-
4 Apr 2016	Payable Credit Note Allocation	Smith & Baker	G/749		160.00	160.00	-
4 Apr 2016	Payable Credit Note Allocation	Smith & Baker	G/749	160.00		(160.00)	-
5 Apr 2016	Payable Invoice	David & Sons	2016-18		13,300.00	13,300.00	-
7 Apr 2016	Payable Invoice	Mark & Tony	A423		2,800.00	2,800.00	-
9 Apr 2016	Payable Invoice	East End Pty Ltd	EE2141		4,400.00	4,400.00	-
11 Apr 2016	Payable Credit Note	David & Sons	2016-18	950.00		(950.00)	-
11 Apr 2016	Payable Credit Note Allocation	David & Sons	2016-18		950.00	950.00	-
11 Apr 2016	Payable Credit Note Allocation	David & Sons	2016-18	950.00		(950.00)	-
28 Apr 2016	Payable Payment	Payment: Gary Corporation	412	5,000.00		(5,000.00)	-
28 Apr 2016	Payable Payment	Payment: Smith & Baker	G/749	1,840.00		(1,840.00)	-
Total Accounts Payable				9,060.00	32,610.00	23,550.00	-
Closing Balance					23,550.00		
Accounts Receivable							
Opening Balance				-			
5 Apr 2016	Receivable Invoice	Horizon Designs	INV-0001	5,235.00		5,235.00	-
10 Apr 2016	Receivable Invoice	Thomson Clothings	INV-0002	3,700.00		3,700.00	-
12 Apr 2016	Receivable Invoice	Globe Travels Pty Ltd	INV-0003	7,880.00		7,880.00	-
13 Apr 2016	Receivable Payment	Payment: Horizon Designs	INV-0001		5,235.00	(5,235.00)	-
14 Apr 2016	Receivable Invoice	Tiffany Cakes	INV-0004	6,090.00		6,090.00	-
17 Apr 2016	Receivable Credit Note	Thomson Clothings	CN-002		700.00	(700.00)	-
17 Apr 2016	Receivable Credit Note Allocation	Thomson Clothings	CN-002	700.00		700.00	-
17 Apr 2016	Receivable Credit Note Allocation	Thomson Clothings	INV-0002		700.00	(700.00)	-
18 Apr 2016	Receivable Payment	Payment: Thomson Clothings	INV-0002		3,000.00	(3,000.00)	-
19 Apr 2016	Receivable Invoice	Peter Electronics	INV-0005	2,300.00		2,300.00	-
20 Apr 2016	Receivable Payment	Payment: Globe Travels Pty Ltd	INV-0003		7,880.00	(7,880.00)	-

Account Transactions

DATE	SOURCE	DESCRIPTION	REFERENCE	DEBIT	CREDIT	GROSS	GST
21 Apr 2016	Receivable Invoice	Sally's Warehouse	INV-0006	7,750.00		7,750.00	-
23 Apr 2016	Receivable Credit Note	Sally's Warehouse	CN-006		150.00	(150.00)	-
23 Apr 2016	Receivable Credit Note Allocation	Sally's Warehouse	CN-006	150.00		150.00	
23 Apr 2016	Receivable Credit Note Allocation	Sally's Warehouse	INV-0006		150.00	(150.00)	
25 Apr 2016	Receivable Payment	Payment: Tiffany Cakes	INV-0004		6,090.00	(6,090.00)	
25 Apr 2016	Receivable Invoice	Western Estate Agents	INV-0007	1,400.00		1,400.00	-
27 Apr 2016	Receivable Invoice	Surf Stores	INV-0008	2,370.00		2,370.00	-
Total Accounts Receivable				**37,575.00**	**23,905.00**	**13,670.00**	**-**
Closing Balance				**13,670.00**			

Bank Fees

DATE	SOURCE	DESCRIPTION	REFERENCE	DEBIT	CREDIT	GROSS	GST
30 Apr 2016	Spend Money	Bank of Richmond - Bank charges	300416	10.00		10.00	-
Total Bank Fees				**10.00**	**-**	**10.00**	**-**

Cleaning

DATE	SOURCE	DESCRIPTION	REFERENCE	DEBIT	CREDIT	GROSS	GST
26 Apr 2016	Spend Money	Melbourne Removals - Cleaning	000006	50.00		55.00	5.00
Total Cleaning				**50.00**	**-**	**55.00**	**5.00**

COGS - A3 Copy Paper

DATE	DESCRIPTION	DEBIT	CREDIT	GROSS	GST
12 Apr 2016	Globe Travels Pty Ltd	1,136.36		1,136.36	-
21 Apr 2016	Sally's Warehouse	1,590.91		1,590.91	-
Total COGS - A3 Copy Paper		**2,727.27**	**-**	**2,727.27**	**-**

COGS - A4 Copy Paper

DATE	DESCRIPTION	DEBIT	CREDIT	GROSS	GST
5 Apr 2016	Horizon Designs	509.09		509.09	-
10 Apr 2016	Thomson Clothings	436.36		436.36	-
12 Apr 2016	Globe Travels Pty Ltd	436.36		436.36	-
14 Apr 2016	Tiffany Cakes	363.64		363.64	-
19 Apr 2016	Peter Electronics	436.36		436.36	-
21 Apr 2016	Sally's Warehouse	509.09		509.09	-
23 Apr 2016	Sally's Warehouse		72.73	(72.73)	-
27 Apr 2016	Surf Stores	363.64		363.64	-
Total COGS - A4 Copy Paper		**3,054.54**	**72.73**	**2,981.81**	**-**

COGS - A5 Copy Paper

DATE	DESCRIPTION	DEBIT	CREDIT	GROSS	GST
5 Apr 2016	Horizon Designs	509.09		509.09	-
25 Apr 2016	Western Estate Agents	727.27		727.27	-
Total COGS - A5 Copy Paper		**1,236.36**	**-**	**1,236.36**	**-**

COGS - Coloured Paper

DATE	DESCRIPTION	DEBIT	CREDIT	GROSS	GST
12 Apr 2016	Globe Travels Pty Ltd	763.64		763.64	-
19 Apr 2016	Peter Electronics	890.91		890.91	-
21 Apr 2016	Sally's Warehouse	763.64		763.64	-
Total COGS - Coloured Paper		**2,418.19**	**-**	**2,418.19**	**-**

Account Transactions | Richmond Papers Pty Ltd

Account Transactions

DATE	SOURCE	DESCRIPTION	REFERENCE	DEBIT	CREDIT	GROSS	GST
COGS - Envelopes Large							
10 Apr 2016		Thomson Clothings		1,600.00		1,600.00	-
14 Apr 2016		Tiffany Cakes		1,200.00		1,200.00	-
17 Apr 2016		Thomson Clothings			400.00	(400.00)	-
Total COGS - Envelopes Large				2,800.00	400.00	2,400.00	-
COGS - Register Rolls							
5 Apr 2016		Horizon Designs		2,072.73		2,072.73	-
12 Apr 2016		Globe Travels Pty Ltd		2,418.18		2,418.18	-
14 Apr 2016		Tiffany Cakes		2,072.73		2,072.73	-
21 Apr 2016		Sally's Warehouse		1,727.27		1,727.27	-
27 Apr 2016		Surf Stores		1,036.36		1,036.36	-
Total COGS - Register Rolls				9,327.27	-	9,327.27	-
Depreciation							
30 Apr 2016	Manual Journal	Depreciation on Motor Vehicle - Depreciation on Motor Vehicle	#71	100.00		100.00	-
Total Depreciation				100.00	-	100.00	-
GST							
Opening Balance					-		
2 Apr 2016	Spend Money	Richmond Real Estate	000002	100.00		(100.00)	-
2 Apr 2016	Spend Money	Western Motors	000001	1,200.00		(1,200.00)	-
2 Apr 2016	Payable Invoice	Gary Corporation	412	454.55		(454.55)	-
2 Apr 2016	Payable Invoice	Smith & Baker	G/749	181.82		(181.82)	-
4 Apr 2016	Payable Invoice	Ian & Co Pty Ltd	00854	363.64		(363.64)	-
4 Apr 2016	Payable Credit Note	Smith & Baker	G/749		14.55	14.55	-
5 Apr 2016	Receivable Invoice	Horizon Designs	INV-0001		475.91	475.91	-
5 Apr 2016	Payable Invoice	David & Sons	2016-18	1,209.09		(1,209.09)	-
7 Apr 2016	Payable Invoice	Mark & Tony	A423	254.55		(254.55)	-
7 Apr 2016	Spend Money	Melbourne Insurance	000003	20.00		(20.00)	-
9 Apr 2016	Payable Invoice	East End Pty Ltd	EE2141	400.00		(400.00)	-
10 Apr 2016	Receivable Invoice	Thomson Clothings	INV-0002		336.37	336.37	-
11 Apr 2016	Payable Credit Note	David & Sons	2016-18		86.36	86.36	-
12 Apr 2016	Receivable Invoice	Globe Travels Pty Ltd	INV-0003		716.37	716.37	-
14 Apr 2016	Receivable Invoice	Tiffany Cakes	INV-0004		553.64	553.64	-
17 Apr 2016	Receivable Credit Note	Thomson Clothings	CN-002	63.64		(63.64)	-
19 Apr 2016	Spend Money	Victoria Electricity	000004	17.67		(17.67)	-
19 Apr 2016	Receivable Invoice	Peter Electronics	INV-0005		209.09	209.09	-
21 Apr 2016	Receivable Invoice	Sally's Warehouse	INV-0006		704.54	704.54	-
21 Apr 2016	Spend Money	Australia Telecom	000005	19.62		(19.62)	-
23 Apr 2016	Receivable Credit Note	Sally's Warehouse	CN-006	13.64		(13.64)	-
25 Apr 2016	Receivable Invoice	Western Estate Agents	INV-0007		127.27	127.27	-

Account Transactions | Richmond Papers Pty Ltd

Account Transactions

DATE	SOURCE	DESCRIPTION	REFERENCE	DEBIT	CREDIT	GROSS	GST
26 Apr 2016	Spend Money	Melbourne Removals	000006	5.00		(5.00)	-
27 Apr 2016	Receivable Invoice	Surf Stores	INV-0008		215.45	215.45	-
Total GST				**4,303.22**	**3,439.55**	**(863.67)**	**-**
Closing Balance				**863.67**			

Insurance

DATE	SOURCE	DESCRIPTION	REFERENCE	DEBIT	CREDIT	GROSS	GST
7 Apr 2016	Spend Money	Melbourne Insurance - Insurance Premium	000003	200.00		220.00	20.00
Total Insurance				**200.00**	**-**	**220.00**	**20.00**

Inventory

DATE	SOURCE	DESCRIPTION	REFERENCE	DEBIT	CREDIT	GROSS	GST
Opening Balance					-		
2 Apr 2016	Payable Invoice	Gary Corporation - A3 Copy Paper	412	4,545.45		5,000.00	454.55
2 Apr 2016	Payable Invoice	Smith & Baker - A5 Copy Paper	G/749	1,818.18		2,000.00	181.82
4 Apr 2016	Payable Invoice	Ian & Co Pty Ltd - A4 Copy Paper	00854	3,636.36		4,000.00	363.64
4 Apr 2016	Payable Credit Note	Smith & Baker - A5 Copy Paper	G/749		145.45	(160.00)	(14.55)
5 Apr 2016	Payable Invoice	David & Sons - Register Rolls	2016-18	12,090.91		13,300.00	1,209.09
5 Apr 2016		Horizon Designs			509.09	(509.09)	-
5 Apr 2016		Horizon Designs			2,072.73	(2,072.73)	-
5 Apr 2016		Horizon Designs			509.09	(509.09)	-
7 Apr 2016	Payable Invoice	Mark & Tony - Coloured Paper	A423	2,545.45		2,800.00	254.55
9 Apr 2016	Payable Invoice	East End Pty Ltd - Envelopes Large	EE2141	4,000.00		4,400.00	400.00
10 Apr 2016		Thomson Clothings			436.36	(436.36)	-
10 Apr 2016		Thomson Clothings			1,600.00	(1,600.00)	-
11 Apr 2016	Payable Credit Note	David & Sons - Register Rolls	2016-18		863.64	(950.00)	(86.36)
12 Apr 2016		Globe Travels Pty Ltd			436.36	(436.36)	-
12 Apr 2016		Globe Travels Pty Ltd			1,136.36	(1,136.36)	-
12 Apr 2016		Globe Travels Pty Ltd			2,418.18	(2,418.18)	-
12 Apr 2016		Globe Travels Pty Ltd			763.64	(763.64)	-
14 Apr 2016		Tiffany Cakes			363.64	(363.64)	-
14 Apr 2016		Tiffany Cakes			2,072.73	(2,072.73)	-
14 Apr 2016		Tiffany Cakes			1,200.00	(1,200.00)	-
17 Apr 2016		Thomson Clothings		400.00		400.00	-
19 Apr 2016		Peter Electronics			436.36	(436.36)	-
19 Apr 2016		Peter Electronics			890.91	(890.91)	-
21 Apr 2016		Sally's Warehouse			509.09	(509.09)	-
21 Apr 2016		Sally's Warehouse			763.64	(763.64)	-
21 Apr 2016		Sally's Warehouse			1,590.91	(1,590.91)	-
21 Apr 2016		Sally's Warehouse			1,727.27	(1,727.27)	-
23 Apr 2016		Sally's Warehouse		72.73		72.73	-
25 Apr 2016		Western Estate Agents			727.27	(727.27)	-
27 Apr 2016		Surf Stores			363.64	(363.64)	-

Account Transactions   Richmond Papers Pty Ltd

Account Transactions

DATE	SOURCE	DESCRIPTION	REFERENCE	DEBIT	CREDIT	GROSS	GST
27 Apr 2016		Surf Stores			1,036.36	(1,036.36)	-
Total Inventory				29,109.08	22,572.72	9,299.10	2,762.74
Closing Balance				6,536.36			

Less Accumulated Depreciation on Motor Vehicle

Opening Balance					-		
30 Apr 2016	Manual Journal	Depreciation on Motor Vehicle - Depreciation on Motor Vehicle	#71		100.00	(100.00)	-
Total Less Accumulated Depreciation on Motor Vehicle				-	100.00	(100.00)	-
Closing Balance					100.00		

Light, Power, Heating

19 Apr 2016	Spend Money	Victoria Electricity - Electricity Bill	000004	176.73		194.40	17.67
Total Light, Power, Heating				176.73	-	194.40	17.67

Motor Vehicle

Opening Balance					-		
2 Apr 2016	Spend Money	Western Motors - Motor vehicle purchased	000001	12,000.00		13,200.00	1,200.00
Total Motor Vehicle				12,000.00	-	13,200.00	1,200.00
Closing Balance				12,000.00			

Owner Funds Introduced

Opening Balance					-		
1 Apr 2016	Receive Money	John Smith - Capital introduced	CR0001		25,000.00	25,000.00	-
Total Owner Funds Introduced				-	25,000.00	25,000.00	-
Closing Balance					25,000.00		

Rent

2 Apr 2016	Spend Money	Richmond Real Estate - Rent	000002	1,000.00		1,100.00	100.00
Total Rent				1,000.00	-	1,100.00	100.00

Richmond Papers Pty Ltd

Opening Balance					-		
1 Apr 2016	Receive Money	John Smith	CR0001	25,000.00		25,000.00	-
2 Apr 2016	Spend Money	Western Motors	000001		13,200.00	(13,200.00)	-
2 Apr 2016	Spend Money	Richmond Real Estate	000002		1,100.00	(1,100.00)	-
7 Apr 2016	Spend Money	Melbourne Insurance	000003		220.00	(220.00)	-
13 Apr 2016	Receivable Payment	Payment: Horizon Designs	Invoice 001	5,235.00		5,235.00	-
18 Apr 2016	Receivable Payment	Payment: Thomson Clothings	Invoice 002	3,000.00		3,000.00	-
19 Apr 2016	Spend Money	Victoria Electricity	000004		194.40	(194.40)	-
20 Apr 2016	Receivable Payment	Payment: Globe Travels Pty Ltd	Invoice 003	7,880.00		7,880.00	-
21 Apr 2016	Spend Money	Australia Telecom	000005		215.84	(215.84)	-
25 Apr 2016	Receivable Payment	Payment: Tiffany Cakes	Invoice 004	6,090.00		6,090.00	-

Account Transactions | Richmond Papers Pty Ltd

Account Transactions

DATE	SOURCE	DESCRIPTION	REFERENCE	DEBIT	CREDIT	GROSS	GST
26 Apr 2016	Spend Money	Melbourne Removals	000006		55.00	(55.00)	-
28 Apr 2016	Payable Payment	Payment: Gary Corporation	000007		5,000.00	(5,000.00)	-
28 Apr 2016	Payable Payment	Payment: Smith & Baker	000008		1,840.00	(1,840.00)	-
30 Apr 2016	Spend Money	Bank of Richmond	300416		10.00	(10.00)	-
Total Richmond Papers Pty Ltd				47,205.00	21,835.24	25,369.76	-
Closing Balance					25,369.76		

Sales - A3 Copy Paper

DATE	SOURCE	DESCRIPTION	REFERENCE	DEBIT	CREDIT	GROSS	GST
12 Apr 2016	Receivable Invoice	Globe Travels Pty Ltd - A3 Copy Paper	INV-0003		1,818.18	2,000.00	181.82
21 Apr 2016	Receivable Invoice	Sally's Warehouse - A3 Copy Paper	INV-0006		2,545.45	2,800.00	254.55
Total Sales - A3 Copy Paper				-	4,363.63	4,800.00	436.37

Sales - A4 Copy Paper

DATE	SOURCE	DESCRIPTION	REFERENCE	DEBIT	CREDIT	GROSS	GST
5 Apr 2016	Receivable Invoice	Horizon Designs - A4 Copy Paper	INV-0001		922.73	1,015.00	92.27
10 Apr 2016	Receivable Invoice	Thomson Clothings - A4 Copy Paper	INV-0002		818.18	900.00	81.82
12 Apr 2016	Receivable Invoice	Globe Travels Pty Ltd - A4 Copy Paper	INV-0003		818.18	900.00	81.82
14 Apr 2016	Receivable Invoice	Tiffany Cakes - A4 Copy Paper	INV-0004		681.82	750.00	68.18
19 Apr 2016	Receivable Invoice	Peter Electronics - A4 Copy Paper	INV-0005		818.18	900.00	81.82
21 Apr 2016	Receivable Invoice	Sally's Warehouse - A4 Copy Paper	INV-0006		954.55	1,050.00	95.45
23 Apr 2016	Receivable Credit Note	Sally's Warehouse - A4 Copy Paper	CN-006	136.36		(150.00)	(13.64)
27 Apr 2016	Receivable Invoice	Surf Stores - A4 Copy Paper	INV-0008		681.82	750.00	68.18
Total Sales - A4 Copy Paper				136.36	5,695.46	6,115.00	555.90

Sales - A5 Copy Paper

DATE	SOURCE	DESCRIPTION	REFERENCE	DEBIT	CREDIT	GROSS	GST
5 Apr 2016	Receivable Invoice	Horizon Designs - A5 Copy Paper	INV-0001		890.91	980.00	89.09
25 Apr 2016	Receivable Invoice	Western Estate Agents - A5 Copy Paper	INV-0007		1,272.73	1,400.00	127.27
Total Sales - A5 Copy Paper				-	2,163.64	2,380.00	216.36

Sales - Coloured Paper

DATE	SOURCE	DESCRIPTION	REFERENCE	DEBIT	CREDIT	GROSS	GST
12 Apr 2016	Receivable Invoice	Globe Travels Pty Ltd - Coloured Paper	INV-0003		1,090.91	1,200.00	109.09
19 Apr 2016	Receivable Invoice	Peter Electronics - Coloured Paper	INV-0005		1,272.73	1,400.00	127.27
21 Apr 2016	Receivable Invoice	Sally's Warehouse - Coloured Paper	INV-0006		1,090.91	1,200.00	109.09
Total Sales - Coloured Paper				-	3,454.55	3,800.00	345.45

Sales - Envelopes Large

DATE	SOURCE	DESCRIPTION	REFERENCE	DEBIT	CREDIT	GROSS	GST
10 Apr 2016	Receivable Invoice	Thomson Clothings - Envelopes Large	INV-0002		2,545.45	2,800.00	254.55

Account Transactions

DATE	SOURCE	DESCRIPTION	REFERENCE	DEBIT	CREDIT	GROSS	GST
14 Apr 2016	Receivable Invoice	Tiffany Cakes - Envelopes Large	INV-0004		1,909.09	2,100.00	190.91
17 Apr 2016	Receivable Credit Note	Thomson Clothings - Envelopes Large	CN-002	636.36		(700.00)	(63.64)
Total Sales - Envelopes Large				**636.36**	**4,454.54**	**4,200.00**	**381.82**

Sales - Register Rolls

DATE	SOURCE	DESCRIPTION	REFERENCE	DEBIT	CREDIT	GROSS	GST
5 Apr 2016	Receivable Invoice	Horizon Designs - Register Rolls	INV-0001		2,945.45	3,240.00	294.55
12 Apr 2016	Receivable Invoice	Globe Travels Pty Ltd - Register Rolls	INV-0003		3,436.36	3,780.00	343.64
14 Apr 2016	Receivable Invoice	Tiffany Cakes - Register Rolls	INV-0004		2,945.45	3,240.00	294.55
21 Apr 2016	Receivable Invoice	Sally's Warehouse - Register Rolls	INV-0006		2,454.55	2,700.00	245.45
27 Apr 2016	Receivable Invoice	Surf Stores - Register Rolls	INV-0008		1,472.73	1,620.00	147.27
Total Sales - Register Rolls				**-**	**13,254.54**	**14,580.00**	**1,325.46**

Telephone & Internet

DATE	SOURCE	DESCRIPTION	REFERENCE	DEBIT	CREDIT	GROSS	GST
21 Apr 2016	Spend Money	Australia Telecom - Telephone Bill	000005	196.22		215.84	19.62
Total Telephone & Internet				**196.22**	**-**	**215.84**	**19.62**

Tracking Transfers

DATE	SOURCE	DESCRIPTION	REFERENCE	DEBIT	CREDIT	GROSS	GST
Opening Balance						-	
4 Apr 2016	Payable Credit Note Allocation	Smith & Baker	G/749	160.00		(160.00)	-
4 Apr 2016	Payable Credit Note Allocation	Smith & Baker	G/749		160.00	160.00	-
11 Apr 2016	Payable Credit Note Allocation	David & Sons	2016-18	950.00		(950.00)	-
11 Apr 2016	Payable Credit Note Allocation	David & Sons	2016-18		950.00	950.00	-
17 Apr 2016	Receivable Credit Note Allocation	Thomson Clothings	CN-002		700.00	700.00	-
17 Apr 2016	Receivable Credit Note Allocation	Thomson Clothings	INV-0002	700.00		(700.00)	-
23 Apr 2016	Receivable Credit Note Allocation	Sally's Warehouse	CN-006		150.00	150.00	-
23 Apr 2016	Receivable Credit Note Allocation	Sally's Warehouse	INV-0006	150.00		(150.00)	-
Total Tracking Transfers				**1,960.00**	**1,960.00**	**-**	**-**
Closing Balance						-	
Total				**165,281.60**	**165,281.60**	**167,986.33**	**7,386.39**

Account Transactions | Richmond Papers Pty Ltd

Bank Reconciliation Summary

Richmond Papers Pty Ltd
Richmond Papers Pty Ltd
As at 30 April 2016

Date	Description	Reference	Amount
30 Apr 2016	Balance in Xero		25,369.76
Plus Outstanding Payments			
26 Apr 2016	Melbourne Removals	000006	55.00
28 Apr 2016	Payment: Smith & Baker	000008	1,840.00
Total Outstanding Payments			**1,895.00**
30 Apr 2016	Statement Balance		27,264.76

Bank Statement

Richmond Papers Pty Ltd
Richmond Papers Pty Ltd
From 1 April 2016 to 30 April 2016

Date	Description	Date imported into Xero	Reference	Reconciled	Source	Amount	Balance
1 Apr 2016	**Opening Balance**						0.00
1 Apr 2016	John Smith	8 May 2016		Yes	Manual	25,000.00	25,000.00
2 Apr 2016	Western Motors	8 May 2016		Yes	Manual	(13,200.00)	11,800.00
2 Apr 2016	Richmond Real Estate	8 May 2016		Yes	Manual	(1,100.00)	10,700.00
7 Apr 2016	Melbourne Insurance	8 May 2016		Yes	Manual	(220.00)	10,480.00
13 Apr 2016	Horizon Designs	8 May 2016		Yes	Manual	5,235.00	15,715.00
18 Apr 2016	Thomson Clothings	8 May 2016		Yes	Manual	3,000.00	18,715.00
19 Apr 2016	Victoria Electricity	8 May 2016		Yes	Manual	(194.40)	18,520.60
20 Apr 2016	Globe Travels Pty Ltd	8 May 2016		Yes	Manual	7,880.00	26,400.60
21 Apr 2016	Australia Telecom	8 May 2016		Yes	Manual	(215.84)	26,184.76
25 Apr 2016	Tiffany Cakes	8 May 2016		Yes	Manual	6,090.00	32,274.76
28 Apr 2016	Gary Corporation	8 May 2016		Yes	Manual	(5,000.00)	27,274.76
30 Apr 2016	Bank of Richmond	8 May 2016		Yes	Manual	(10.00)	27,264.76
	Closing Balance						**27,264.76**

Bank Reconciliation | Richmond Papers Pty Ltd   As at 30 April 2016   Page 2 of 3

Statement Exceptions

Richmond Papers Pty Ltd
Richmond Papers Pty Ltd
From 1 April 2016 to 30 April 2016

Date	Description	Reference	Reconciled	Source	Reason	Amount
1 Apr 2016	John Smith		Yes	Manual	Manual	25,000.00
2 Apr 2016	Western Motors		Yes	Manual	Manual	(13,200.00)
2 Apr 2016	Richmond Real Estate		Yes	Manual	Manual	(1,100.00)
7 Apr 2016	Melbourne Insurance		Yes	Manual	Manual	(220.00)
13 Apr 2016	Horizon Designs		Yes	Manual	Manual	5,235.00
18 Apr 2016	Thomson Clothings		Yes	Manual	Manual	3,000.00
19 Apr 2016	Victoria Electricity		Yes	Manual	Manual	(194.40)
20 Apr 2016	Globe Travels Pty Ltd		Yes	Manual	Manual	7,880.00
21 Apr 2016	Australia Telecom		Yes	Manual	Manual	(215.84)
25 Apr 2016	Tiffany Cakes		Yes	Manual	Manual	6,090.00
28 Apr 2016	Gary Corporation		Yes	Manual	Manual	(5,000.00)
30 Apr 2016	Bank of Richmond		Yes	Manual	Manual	(10.00)

Statement of Cash Flows

Richmond Papers Pty Ltd
For the month ended 30 April 2016

	APR 2016
Cash Flows from Operating Activities	
Receipts from customers	22,205.00
Payments to suppliers and employees	(15,029.54)
Cash receipts from other operating activities	(1,821.82)
Total Cash Flows from Operating Activities	**5,353.64**
Cash Flows from Investing Activities	
Other cash items from investing activities	(4,983.88)
Total Cash Flows from Investing Activities	**(4,983.88)**
Cash Flows from Financing Activities	
Other cash items from financing activities	25,000.00
Total Cash Flows from Financing Activities	**25,000.00**
Net Cash Flows	**25,369.76**
Cash Balances	
Cash and cash equivalents at beginning of period	-
Cash and cash equivalents at end of period	25,369.76
Net change in cash for period	**25,369.76**

Trial Balance

Richmond Papers Pty Ltd
As at 30 April 2016

Account	Debit	Credit	YTD Debit	YTD Credit
Revenue				
Sales - A3 Copy Paper (201)		4,364		4,364
Sales - A4 Copy Paper (202)		5,559		5,559
Sales - A5 Copy Paper (203)		2,164		2,164
Sales - Coloured Paper (204)		3,455		3,455
Sales - Envelopes Large (205)		3,818		3,818
Sales - Register Rolls (206)		13,255		13,255
Expenses				
Bank Fees (404)	10		10	
Cleaning (408)	50		50	
COGS - A3 Copy Paper (311)	2,727		2,727	
COGS - A4 Copy Paper (312)	2,982		2,982	
COGS - A5 Copy Paper (313)	1,236		1,236	
COGS - Coloured Paper (314)	2,418		2,418	
COGS - Envelopes Large (315)	2,400		2,400	
COGS - Register Rolls (316)	9,327		9,327	
Depreciation (416)	100		100	
Insurance (433)	200		200	
Light, Power, Heating (445)	177		177	
Rent (469)	1,000		1,000	
Telephone & Internet (489)	196		196	
Assets				
Accounts Receivable (610)	13,670		13,670	
Inventory (630)	6,536		6,536	
Motor Vehicle (730)	12,000		12,000	
Less Accumulated Depreciation on Motor Vehicle (731)		100		100
Richmond Papers Pty Ltd	25,370		25,370	
Liabilities				
Accounts Payable (800)		23,550		23,550
GST (820)	864		864	
Owner Funds Introduced (881)		25,000		25,000
Total	**81,264**	**81,264**	**81,264**	**81,264**

Profit & Loss

Richmond Papers Pty Ltd
1 April 2016 to 30 April 2016

	30 Apr 16
Income	
Sales - A3 Copy Paper	4,364
Sales - A4 Copy Paper	5,559
Sales - A5 Copy Paper	2,164
Sales - Coloured Paper	3,455
Sales - Envelopes Large	3,818
Sales - Register Rolls	13,255
Total Income	**32,614**
Less Cost of Sales	
COGS - A3 Copy Paper	2,727
COGS - A4 Copy Paper	2,982
COGS - A5 Copy Paper	1,236
COGS - Coloured Paper	2,418
COGS - Envelopes Large	2,400
COGS - Register Rolls	9,327
Total Cost of Sales	**21,091**
Gross Profit	**11,523**
Less Operating Expenses	
Bank Fees	10
Cleaning	50
Depreciation	100
Insurance	200
Light, Power, Heating	177
Rent	1,000
Telephone & Internet	196
Total Operating Expenses	**1,733**
Net Profit	**9,790**

Balance Sheet

Richmond Papers Pty Ltd
As at 30 April 2016

	30 Apr 2016
Assets	
Bank	
Richmond Papers Pty Ltd	25,370
Total Bank	**25,370**
Current Assets	
Accounts Receivable	13,670
Inventory	6,536
Total Current Assets	**20,206**
Non-current Assets	
Motor Vehicle	12,000
Less Accumulated Depreciation on Motor Vehicle	(100)
Total Non-current Assets	**11,900**
Total Assets	**57,476**
Liabilities	
Current Liabilities	
Accounts Payable	23,550
GST	(864)
Owner Funds Introduced	25,000
Total Current Liabilities	**47,686**
Total Liabilities	**47,686**
Net Assets	**9,790**
Equity	
Current Year Earnings	9,790
Total Equity	**9,790**